Nine Changes of The Watery Star

Collected Poems by Andrew Buchanan Vol 4

Arts Agency

Published in the United Kingdom
by The Arts Agency 2020
ISBN 978-0-9564799-7-6

Andrew Buchanan
has asserted his right under the
Copyrights, Designs and Patents Act 1988
to be identified as the author of this work.
Poems Copyright © Andrew Buchanan 2020

Other books published by The Arts Agency include:

'A Chain of Stars' Sanae Morita
ISBN 978-0-9564799-0-7

'Days Like Leaves'
Collected Poems by
Andrew Buchanan
ISBN 978-0-9564799-4-5

'Tangled Hair'
Collected Poems by
Andrew Buchanan Vol 2
ISBN 978-0-9564799-5-2

'New Southampton Poets'
Andrew Buchanan, Dave Hubble
Kayleigh O'Reilly, Damian O'Vitich,
Angelia Saplan, Stewart Taylor
ISBN 978-0-9564799-6-9

'a night of stars'
Collected Poems by
Andrew Buchanan Vol 3
ISBN 978-0-9564799-2-1

Published and Designed by The Arts Agency
www.artsagency.co.uk

THANK YOU MARCH!

Andy :)

Dedicated to you for buying this book....

Titles

Christmas Poem

Walking along the road
Past the homeless guys
and the pretty girls
wrapped up warmly in wool

I see the lights under the stars,
hanging from the
black tree branches and lampposts
Shining glowing golden and
purest brightest white

These are my gold and silver
this Christmas in the city at night

winter city

And it's cold in
November in the park
As winter chill comes in
under tilting nights
in the winter city

The cars crawl home

The cars crawl home
in the darkening night

She waits against the window
for a long time

He walks along the path
In the drizzle that
turns to a downpour

It's the price we pay
for someone we love

In the city
in the rain
at night

an armful of stars

My friend
she's a dancer

And sometimes
when she reaches up
she elegantly takes
a handful, and then another,
until she holds
an armful of stars

Burning brightly and oh so hot
but soothed by the
coolness of her touch

Then concentrating
hard momentarily
with her mouth half open
and her tongue curled

She then folds them
carefully into her pocket
And then smiles at me
as if to say
Look what I can do

And what gets me
about this girl
Is that she has
All the charm in the world

But unless you
know her and she trusts you
she somehow keeps it hidden
in baggy dresses and old jumpers
to protect herself

But, maybe, it's
also to protect you,
from falling for her
as easily as
she takes her stars

after the rains

In the city
after the rains
It seems like
anything is
possible again

And when there's not much light in the sky

And when there's
not much light in the sky
a few flickering stars
obscured by clouds

And I feel it's how
this night should be
as under the broken
stars and streetlights we go

In search of our muse
for whom we are
just the amanuensis
However she comes,
in whatever form she takes

As the night rolls to one side
And we turn into
somewhere quite different
Where we have never been

And the old dreams are
replaced by new ones
And time stops
if only for a moment

A constant star

She is like a constant star
brighter than all the rest

Burning hot and cold
Illuminating all she sees

But she is so far beyond me
she is out of my reach

All the light in the room

She captures
all the light in the room
And bends it around herself
Without even trying

Because, like you and me,
it wants to be near her
As if it too cannot escape
the gravity of her beauty

a time of small things

It was a time of small things
but with fearful consequences
In our lost midnights
and wishful rainy days
when we daren't even go
outside the door

My days are colourless
and it seems like
all our tomorrows
have been cancelled
for an indefinite
and uncertain future

But, in my heart
the spring winds
are already blowing

And as the singing of my ghosts

And as the
singing of my ghosts
Calls out ineluctably
and unassailably to me

I wonder,
when did the road change
from looking forward
to a brighter tomorrow,
to looking back at
a better yesterday?

But maybe it's because
I am always good at leaving,
even before I have arrived

Or we have made wrong turns
or luck has dealt us not so much
So that what was once forever,
is now a rapidly shortening
tunnel into the end

But now, because of you
My ghosts take flight
And maybe I have
something of a future
As your sunlight
chases my ghosts away

Caramel

Your light
brown skin
like caramel

Your corkscrew
blonde curls
tumble down
like a carousel

Your bright
green eyes
whose secrets
I cannot tell

And my head
is full of you

And maybe

And maybe,
like a paper aeroplane
trying to reach the moon,
I was hoping for too much

That someone as beautiful as you
with all the natural assumptions
that beauty brings
Your almost supernatural poise
and heartbreaking smile

But I certainly know now
as I spend my days in numb despair
As I live through empty stories
none of which contain you

And the world is reduced

And the world is reduced
To her breath on my chest
and the beat of her heart

to just you and me
when two become one

If only for her

I remember her
her small firm breasts

She was like
a shower of pure light
Whose mere presence
washed you clean of all sadness

And made you yearn to be
a better person

if only for her

Will find a way

And so she says
Love will find a way for us

But I am not so sure
A way where, I wonder
But daren't ask

But you touch
every place in my heart
in ways which I had forgotten
or not dared hope for

And so perhaps that is
more than enough

And in the ending of anything

And in the ending of anything
there is always
something that remains

A kind of sadness,
for people and places we have
loved and laughed and shared

And for
what will now
be no more

Even you and I

Even you and I
as we lurch unconscionably
to some kind of quiescence
But this annulment of differences
Never lasts

For it seems we have been
individuals for too long
to sacrifice too much
too soon and too blindly

For an uncertain alliance that
while not without its benefits,
takes too heavy a toll on
our freedom loving natures
or selfishness, call it what you will

And our wishes, fears
and deep desires
to be ineluctably untrammeled
and left alone in peace

I have noticed something

I have noticed something
The women I seem to be drawn to
are all bright, beautiful,
and, perhaps, just a little crazy

As if their dreams are
too big for this world,
As if their life is
somehow incomplete,
And it makes me feel like
I want to help them

I suppose I am also
searching for something,
for some kind of
acknowledgement or affection

Two broken people
half connecting
in the night

I have heard the angels singing

I have heard
the angels singing
Boy she's not for you

And I saw my girl dancing
And she said Don't you
know we're through

And she has the armour
of her beauty and grace
inviolate and beyond me

When your heart is full of rain,
and love no longer is for you

night's black palace

And under
night's black palace
where the stars
pierce the blackness

She's like a dark flower
burning bright
As she burns through
all my solitude
like a falling star

Pretty Girl

Pretty girl
On her way home

Determinately hurrying
through the darkening streets
Head bowed down

Long hair and coat
Swirling behind her
Crutching her bag
closely to her bosom

Don't you just wish
it was you she was
taking home instead

Our own sky and heaven

And so she said to me
Let us create
our own sky and heaven

Where the day meets the night
Where the sun meets the moon

And I said
where have you been
for so long

And she replied
on the other side
of the world
and far away

But let us go
because
it's our time now

when the streets empty
and the lights go out
one by one by one

Obon

On the festival of Obon
the Buddhist Day of the Dead
which lasts for the three days

Lanterns are hung outside houses
to guide the spirits of the ancestors home
Graves are cleaned and food is offered
Gunpowder drifts past like perfume

How sorry I am
The Japanese do more
for their deceased parents
in their afterlife
Than I ever did for mine
when they were alive

Nights of Winter Rain

In these cities of night
under a rain soaked moon

We come and go
scurry for shelter
And look and see
searching for something
uncertain in intention
but still important to us

But which we sadly
never really seem to find,
Only suggestions of
echoes of the past
and lost futures

Because sad and careful
creatures that we are

We all know that
the past is the land to which
We can never return

Slow Boat

I take the
slow boat to sleep
But usually in the
wrong time and place

After a hard day's
working, travelling
and then eating

I then wake up
drowsy and confused
on my sofa

But now I have to
lie awake, through the
whole river of night

Sleep is a boat
that sails off
once a night

And try as you might
you can never
board her again
without paying
a price

At the edge of winter

We're at the edge of winter now
The summer sun no longer shines
The leaves no longer
strewn picturesquely around
in their rustling russet
carpets of autumn,
and so forth

But now, in this psychotic winter
I look up at the stars
While in my city full of sigils, artifacts,
and signposts to lost causes
We walk around like broken toys

And soon
the darkness of midnight
flows through my veins

When something inside
so deeply denied
finally recognises itself
in someone or something else

While at
the same time
I realise that
starlight still falls
upon my house
all the time

And through we go

And through these
ancient city gates we go
flanked by lions rampant

As the tides come silently in
An empty sail takes the wind

And feral dreams stir unbidden
from somewhere long forgotten

And I see

And I see
across the shining black water
The bright city lights
where I have never been
And never will go

And I see the pretty girls
laughing on buses
Whom beyond a shy smile
I will never know

And I see
outside my curtains
that the morning
is trying to get in

That's all I can ask for really
And maybe, just maybe
that's enough for now

She baked me cakes for my birthday

She baked me
cakes for my birthday
and danced at my parties

I always thought the world of her
and so did everyone else
With good reason
Intelligent, attentive, kind,
beautiful and funny
Even my straight women
friends wanted her

I always adored you
but considered you to be
out of my reach
Like the beautiful brave girl
on the highwire
way up high above us

When I saw you last you posted on fb,
Running on my way to see Andy,
the only person who believed in me
And I was so happy I can't describe it

Now you have gone back home,
taking your new baby but the
sometimes but useless father not in tow

I realise what I have missed,
how much you meant to me,
and many others as well
How I took for granted
you would always be there

But now you have gone

I sometimes don't know what
the difference between
love and being in love is
I loved you as did everyone

But if there is a
boundary between the two
With you I think I could
have already crossed it

The first time I saw you

The first time I saw you
I knew you were the one
who was too good for me

This day has

This day has
got away from me
And I've barely begun

But it's inclement October
and the sky is full of rain
My ghosts move in in tight array
And another day just fades away

And under black skies

And under black skies
with missing stars
We go on

Consult our charts
on the way to
Who knows where or what
stolen light but death

Under stars that
now suddenly
wheel faster
than they should
I came low
to come home

In the shade of evening

In the shade of evening
early while the sun sinks slowly

We sip wine, make smart remarks
and laugh and talk of whatever we like
And don't think of what is to come

And then
after the edge of light
has diminished into darkness

Then we go out
into the black night
under spattered stars

In search of the
answers to questions
we dare not even ask

We talk our little noises

We talk our little noises
and dream our little dreams
And if we are very lucky
we can work to make them real

And if we make them real
sometimes we sometimes find
that it doesn't really help that much
when the world is so unkind

For it seems

For it seems
These are the days we live now
Independent but unassured
as the sky turns again and again
But still nothing changes much
for the better or for the worse

And it seems
I have become
lost to the world,
in which I otherwise
wasted so much time,
is a tired but
sadly true song

Night's Companion

She's dressed in shadows
at the other end of the room

And I still cannot help myself
but acutely sense everything about her
She's like a dark star that eclipses
everything else in my senses

Her perfume a dark scent
like a flower that
only blooms at night
She comes to me
smiling secretly to herself
pleased with her beauty

And as her dark hair
sways down the arch of her pale back
she places her cool fingers
on the nape of my neck
to draw me to her
and to softly whisper in my ear
all the things she wants

And so I think to myself
while I am still capable of thinking,
dear god, her cool skin, her passion,
as she hotly flowers in the darkness
and takes me past all desire, past all need

Seeking comfort

Seeing comfort
in the familiar
and what we know

For the world
and the people in it,
including myself,
are really, when
all is said and done,
too indifferent to care

And the effort it takes
is very sadly often
too much for
too little return

Lying awake at night

Lying awake at night
thinking about things

A fraying patchwork
of possibilities that are
probably really
only improbabilities

But never really able
to decide on anything
Aimlessly fretting for
a long and restless time

Until suddenly
unwelcome and unbidden
four am comes to call

And I can see

And I can see
in the sudden
sweet silence
of this new
born morning

The gently
malingering moon
still visible in the
bright light blue
early morning sky

As if she
doesn't really
want to go
just yet

Saturday Morning

And, in a bright room called morning
I get up, put the linen in the washing machine,
and have a leisurely bath

And, at least for this morning,
I don't have to worry and fret about
what has been or has still to come

I put on my veggie breakfast
And while it is cooking
put the fresh washing out on the line.

And then, after this
uncharacteristically virtuous start,
I then sit and read and
eat my breakfast outside,
like a gentleman of leisure
in my sunlit city courtyard

While thinking about
all the things to do,
or even better, those which I
can happily postpone

And the possible pleasures
of the whole day and evening
stretching way ahead of me
and of the days still to come

Old Friends

We agree to meet up again.
You both make a special effort
to come all the way to my city
for which I am eternally grateful

I remember you were both women
in unhappy marriages and relationships
and you both confided in me,
their short comings, your unhappiness,
and your affairs

Now you are both happier.
One happily married, saying
to us in all seriousness
"Isn't it terrible when you
actually like your husband"
And then we all burst out laughing
The other after years of being used by men
is now thank god happily non committal -
saying "It'll end when I want it to end"
and "I'll leave him when I want to"

And I wonder after so many years
what you have both moved on
And I have stayed the same
What is this bond and affection
we have for each other, because it is still there

Maybe it's because we are
old friends until the end.

Sustained by

And, sustained by the
fragile uncertainties of love,
we shall play, for
tomorrow and today

Until the moon turns
against the silver stars
And night reclaims
its lovers once again

Spring scatters

And as Spring scatters her
sunlit clouds and showers
we fall gently asleep

And when we wake
we see that above us
The shining stars have
shifted across
their entire axes
Whole constellations
and galaxies have
turned in their
immense dreaming aeons

For it seems that
as well as her
soft warm rains,
Spring also scatters
her brilliant stars
right across our
visible heavens

Poetry Readings

This pretty girl poet
she said to me
I wish I could read like you

Because whenever you read
you shut the whole room down
as you create this atmosphere
of quiet intimacy and intensity
that just takes me in
Completely

I tell her I am
really touched
that she says this,
which is true
I am

I tell her
I like her work too
At least as much of it as
I can actually make out

Because she reads too quickly
mumbles into her phone
and away from the microphone

And so half the time
I can never unfortunately
hear what she is saying

Which is a shame
because what she is saying
is, at least as far as I can tell,
pretty good

But I can tell
she doesn't know
whether to believe me or not
And, if so, why would none
of her friends not already
have told her this ?
Something which I
also completely fail to
understand as well
And so, this is not really
what she wants to hear

But, mostly I am just
happy to hear that
anyone actually
listens to me
at all

Hello October

Well Hello October
I see you've come to
pretty constantly
rain on me again

To let me know that I have,
somehow, once again,
managed to miss
yet another summer,
with her expansive long,
golden and dreaming days,
for good this time

For, as we look up at the sky
from the depths of the city,
no matter how wide
the sky may be,
peering up, we can only
ever see a small square of sky
that's in front of us,
and way out of reach

As the prospect
of the forthcoming
darkness of winter
looms over us all
once again

And nothing is

And when
all your days
are yesterdays
nothing is as it
ever was again

And the future
disappears
tightly constrained
secretly lost

And the silence
listens for a song
But it never comes

So turning indoors
you stay inside
avoid the world
and seek shelter
from the
coming storms

As floating clouds

As floating clouds
- Scatter -
slowly but surely
apart

Deep within
my own space
The days of
my life pass
But more slowly

And it seems
as if it is
more under
my control

But you know
fairly soon
Time will tell
And I've already
spent a lot of that

But I suppose
the trick is to
learn how to live in
the heart of this world
and its collapsing empires

But not be of it

All in its season?

They say
Life passes
All in its season

But I have never fit in
I always had to create
my own spaces to be

Never doing
what I should
Ignoring the years
And more

But I am out of step
I always have been
And I don't know why
But your world made
little or no sense to me

And so I turned away
and made my own
for me and others
like me, broken
but still hopeful

Always
out of step
And sadly
soon to be
out of time

Darkest stars

From the darkest stars
to the darkest days
they come relentlessly

and you know
there is never really any escape
no matter how you try

your days are marked
and around the next corner,
or the one after that,
death has your name

We have

silver stars for our nights
a golden star for our days
and black stars for our dreams